In Memory of:

Julia Stuppy Geesa

from

Ella Stuppy Buchanan

When the Greatest Show on Earth Rode the Rails

THE CIRCUS COMES HOME

By **Lois Duncan**

Photographs by **Joseph Janney Steinmetz**

A Doubleday Book for Young Readers

A Doubleday Book for Young Readers
Published by
Delacorte Press
Bantam Doubleday Dell Publishing Group, Inc.
1540 Broadway
New York, New York 10036
Doubleday and the portrayal of an anchor with a dolphin are trademarks of
Bantam Doubleday Dell Publishing Group, Inc.
Text copyright © 1993 by Lois Duncan
All photographs by Joseph Janney Steinmetz
Front cover photograph: Four famous clowns (clockwise from left): Felix
Adler, Emmett Kelly, Harry Dann, and Paul Jerome.

Library of Congress Cataloging in Publication Data

Duncan, Lois
The circus comes home / by Lois Duncan; photos by Joseph
Janney Steinmetz.
Includes index.
      p.   cm.
Summary: Photographs and text chronicle the history of the Ringling
brothers' circus, which toured the United States until 1956, describing such
acts as the Flying Wallendas and the Elephant Ballet.
ISBN 0-385-30689-X
1. Circus—Juvenile literature.   [1. Ringling Bros.–History.
2. Circus—History.]   I. Steinmetz, Joseph Janney, ill.   II. Title.
GV1817.D86   1993
791.3—dc20   92-7481   CIP   AC

Design by Lynn Braswell
Manufactured in the United States of America
October 1993
10 9 8 7 6 5 4 3 2 1

LOIS DUNCAN grew up in Sarasota, Florida, when that town was the winter quarters for the Ringling brothers' circus. She knew from early childhood that she wanted to be a writer and began submitting stories to magazines at age ten. Her first story was published when she was thirteen, and she wrote her first young adult novel when she was twenty. Today she is the award-winning author of forty books, and the recipient of the American Library Association's Margaret A. Edwards Award, which honors the body of work of a young adult novelist.

JOSEPH JANNEY STEINMETZ, Duncan's father, began his career as a photographer in the 1920s with such magazines as *Life, Holiday,* and *The Saturday Evening Post.* He was later to become renowned as a social historian who chronicled American life during the 1930s and 1940s. Shortly before his death in 1985, major shows of Steinmetz's work were exhibited in Paris, at the Carpenter Center for the Visual Arts at Harvard, and at the International Center of Photography in New York. His personal favorite pictures were those that depicted "The Golden Age of Circus."

In memory of my photographer father,
Joseph Janney Steinmetz,
a man who captured magic

After a seven-month tour of the country, the Ringling
Bros. and Barnum & Bailey circus train returns to
winter quarters in Sarasota, Florida.

Once upon a time—when the ground was made of sawdust, and people in spangled tights flew through the air like birds, and elephants dressed in tutus and danced on their toes—there was magic in our land.

That magic was *circus*. And the greatest circus of all was the Ringling Bros. and Barnum & Bailey, with sixteen hundred troupers and a menagerie of animals from twenty-eight countries.

Seven months of each year Ringling Bros. toured the United States, covering twenty thousand miles and giving performances in some one hundred forty cities. Then when winter set in and the summertime spectators huddled at home in front of their fireplaces, the circus band played "Auld Lang Syne" to indicate that the season was over, and the circus returned to its home in Sarasota, Florida.

I was a child back then, and we lived in Sarasota. My father, Joseph Steinmetz, was a professional photographer at a time when very few people had cameras of their own. He was also a magician who delighted in special effects, such as plucking coins out of the air and making elephants spring out of laundry baskets. The first time my father saw a clown he fell in love with the circus, and his greatest joy was recording its magic on film.

OPPOSITE: Photographer Joseph Steinmetz was also a magician who delighted in special effects.

Author Lois Duncan spent her childhood in Sarasota, Florida, during "The Golden Age of Circus."

The first three sections of the circus train were timed to arrive at each new location at daybreak so the big top could be erected and the seating installed in time for a noon show. Two dining tents were also erected, one for the managers and performers to eat in and the other for the workmen.

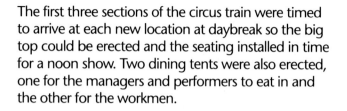

The Ringling Bros. circus train was actually composed of four trains. The section to arrive first at every location was known as "The Flying Squadron," and it carried everything necessary to lay out the lot for the show and to set up the cook houses. It also carried the kitchen and dining room equipment and a staff of 174 cook people, who immediately set to work preparing breakfast, so that a hot meal would be waiting for the work crew when they arrived to set up the tents.

The second section carried the animals and their attendants, and the canvas and poles for the big top. The third brought the contents of the big top, including the lighting, rigging, and seating for twelve thousand people, while the fourth section brought the officials and all the performers.

OPPOSITE: The roustabouts who did the heavy labor of setting up and tearing down the tents and moving the equipment often traveled eighty men to the train car. Each was given four buckets of cold water per day to wash in, two in the morning and two at night.

BELOW LEFT: The Tattooed Lady, Betty Broadbent, dresses in the cramped quarters of the circus train restroom.

BELOW: Harry Dann, shown here with one of the show girls, was famous as a White Face Clown, but he also served as schoolteacher for the circus children while the show was on tour.

Everybody who toured with the circus had a berth in a sleeping car. The top officials had their own private railroad cars, and the highest-ranking performers and their families had staterooms with kitchen areas and couches that folded down into beds. The roustabouts, who loaded and unloaded the equipment and erected the tents, slept in three-tier bunks. The midgets slept in baby beds; the giant had an extra-long berth; and the fat lady squeezed her double-width body into an almost double-width sleeping area.

BELOW: The Doll family of midgets—Daisy, Tiny, Gracie, and Harry—entertain themselves playing poker in one of the train berths.

OPPOSITE: The Fat Lady, Alice from Dallas, relaxes with a magazine on the train and snacks on dog biscuits. In early years the Fat Lady's salary was determined by her weight. She had to weigh in every payday and received fifty cents per pound.

14

Returning to winter
quarters in Florida
meant fun in
the sun for circus
performers.

The return to winter quarters was exciting for everyone. Performers might go to sleep with a blizzard raging outside the train windows and wake up to the sight of palm trees and the smell of orange blossoms. For the next five months they would relax, rest up from their travels, develop new acts, and rehearse outside in the sunshine.

Acrobats relax and rehearse in the winter quarters backyard.

The winter quarters were set up on a two-hundred-acre lot that had once been the city fairgrounds. John Ringling, the youngest of the five brothers who founded the circus, laid out the quarters in 1927, with workshops, horse barns, cages, and pens for the menagerie, an elephant house, a railroad shop, and an outdoor rehearsal arena that was the exact same size as the one in Madison Square Garden, where the circus always staged its first performance of the season.

The winter quarters were always open to the public. Anybody who wanted to visit the menagerie, the blacksmith shop, and the outdoor rehearsal areas could do so and could chat with the performers who congregated in the circus backyard.

For circus children, "coming home" meant a total change of life-style. Although they enjoyed the excitement of touring with their parents, they never stayed in any one place long enough to get to know the town and form any friendships there. While on tour they seldom got to bed before midnight, since the performers' section of the train was the last to leave each performance site, and they were rocked to sleep by the lurch of rumbling train cars. Their meals were served at community tables in a cook tent known as the "Hotel Ringling," and their schooling took place in the backyard areas of circus lots, where they were tutored by one of the clowns.

Karl Wallenda starts his daughter, Carla, age five, across a twenty-foot-high wire. Although they're not in the photograph, there were "about eighteen uncles" standing beneath her to catch her if she fell. Carla made her first public appearance at age three, when she rode on her father's shoulders as he walked the high wire in Palisades Park, New Jersey.

Ten years later Carla was a regular part of the act. Today Carla owns and performs in her own small circus and is training her grandchildren to walk the high wire.

Karl Wallenda installed a wire-walking rig in the yard
behind his home so he and his family could rehearse
whenever they felt like it.

In Sarasota they lived in houses and attended regular
schools. Even so, their lives were different from those of
their classmates, because most performers expected their
children to follow in their footsteps. They trained them
into the family acts from babyhood, and instead of giving
them sandboxes and swings for play equipment, they pro-
vided them with trapezes, trampolines, and tightwires.

One of the best known of the circus families was the Wallendas. The father, Karl, and the rest of the large, extended family developed the most chilling high-wire act in the world. They performed on a tightwire forty feet in the air without using a safety net and weren't content just to walk on it; they stood on their heads, pedaled across it on bicycles, and climbed on each other's shoulders to form three-layer pyramids. Since heat could affect the tension of the performing wire, Karl carried a thermometer when he performed and kept constant check on the temperature at the top of the tent.

The Ringlings brought the Wallenda family over from Germany. When they made their first appearance in the United States, the crowd was so overwhelmed by their incredible act that they gave them a standing ovation, applauding and stomping their feet as if they'd gone crazy. In Europe, a noisy reaction meant people didn't like you, and the broken-hearted performers thought their act was a failure. They slunk back to their dressing room, changed out of their costumes, and started making plans to return to their homeland. Then the ringmaster rushed back to give them the happy news that in America people applauded to show their approval. The audience continued to clap for a quarter of an hour while the Wallendas got back into their costumes and returned to the center ring to take their bows.

Richard Guzman, Carla's husband; Raymond Chitty,
a young man they were training; Karl Wallenda;
Carla Wallenda.

This daredevil family was not immune to accidents. During a heavy rain in 1934, while Karl, his wife Helen, and brothers Hermann and Joseph were up on the high wire, the wet ground started to sink, and the wire went slack just as Helen was climbing onto Karl's shoulders. Wire walkers train themselves always to fall forward, to give themselves a chance to grab hold of the wire. Hermann caught the wire, and Joseph grabbed Hermann. Karl also managed to grab on to the wire, and as Helen plummeted past him he stretched out his legs and caught her head between his ankles. With Joseph still clinging to his legs Hermann went hand over hand to the platform, while Karl continued to hold Helen's head in a scissors grip until a safety net could be set up below them.

Miraculously none of them was injured.

In 1962 the Wallendas were far less lucky. This time the family was performing as a seven-person pyramid, when Karl's nephew, Dieter Schepp, who was new to the group, lost his grip on his balance pole and caused the whole pyramid to collapse. Dieter and Karl's son-in-law, Richard Faughan, were killed in the fall, and Karl's son, Mario, was crippled for life.

Three days later the survivors were up on the wire again.

The Wallendas didn't use safety nets for two reasons. The reason they voiced publicly was that it was dangerous to fall into a net among bicycles and balance beams. But their real reason was psychological. If you think you're going to survive, you're less afraid to fall, and a fall would destroy their act.

A thrill-seeker to the end, Karl Wallenda died at age seventy-three on March 22, 1978, in San Juan, Puerto Rico. He was walking a 750-foot wire stretched between two hotels when a gust of wind blew him off and he fell twelve stories to his death. Two years later Carla Wallenda's son, Enrico, returned to San Juan and completed the walk that killed his grandfather.

While the Wallendas practiced their act on a rig in their backyard, other aerialists were rehearsing at the winter quarters practice grounds. It was there that the Flying Concellos and the huge, multitalented Cristiani family soared and spun and somersaulted through space while they deepened their tans in the warmth of the Florida sunshine.

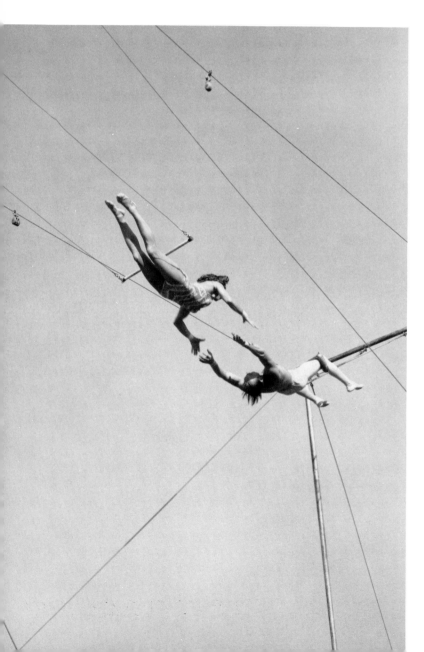

The greatest challenge for aerialists was to work together as a unit. At the top of the tent they had to perform as one person, for if their timing was a fraction of a second off, it could very well mean death. Although the flyer received the applause, the catcher was the most important member of the team. It was he who had to gauge his swing to put him in the right spot at exactly the right time to receive the flyer.

There were so many Cristianis performing with Ringling Bros. that they had their own train car with their name painted on it. This family consisted not only of trapeze artists but of tumblers, jugglers, and equestrians. The bareback riders were renowned for their heart-stopping "Suicide Act," during which three men circled the ring on galloping horses and did simultaneous somersaults through hoops, each one landing on the back of the horse behind him.

OPPOSITE: Handlers put circus horses through their paces.

BELOW: Ralph Alexander Clark, a circus rider in uniform, takes his horse over a jump.

With acrobatic riding, timing was critical. The rider had to be certain all the horses would retain the exact same speed so that the animal he leapt to would be positioned to provide a secure landing field. The most important thing for a ring horse to learn was to hold a steady pace, no matter what happened to him. Their trainers tied tin cans to the horses' tails, fired revolvers into the air to startle them, and darted out from the sidelines, waving and shouting, to teach the horses to disregard distractions. To keep the performers from slipping, the backs of the horses were coated with resin powder, which is why trick horses are referred to as "resinbacks" or "rosinbacks."

Belemonte Cristiani, of the famous family of equestrians, helps lead his horse, Rube, to the veterinarian hospital. Rube broke his foreleg taking a jump.

Clown Prince
Paul Jerome,
a great admirer
of the Cristianis,
enjoyed watching
them rehearse.

Another exciting animal act was the "Cat Act," which featured the great French animal trainer, Alfred Court. Court prided himself on controlling his animals with kindness and refused to take a chair or a gun into the cage with him. He specialized in mixing species that were deadly enemies and on one occasion had eight lions, three polar bears, two black bears, two leopards, two wolves, two dogs, and a jaguar in the same cage. Another of his acts involved twelve tigers who performed in a cage with six "terrified" show girls.

Court always ended his act by strolling around the arena with a leopard draped around his neck.

Only one of every five lions was smart enough to be trained into the act; the others served as "window dressing." Lions born in the wild were safer to work with than those who were born in captivity, because they had more fear and respect for man. The cats were fed sixteen pounds of horsemeat a day, supplemented by milk and raw eggs. One problem for Alfred Court was that his lions got to like him and wanted to play with him. A playful lion is dangerous because a friendly pat with a sharp-clawed paw can rake a trainer's face off.

Although tigers were more intelligent than lions, they were more dangerous to work with, because they had faster reflexes. The deadliest animals of all to work with were bears, because they didn't bite and let go. If a bear got hold of his trainer, he tore him apart.

The "Cat Act" was generally the opening act at each performance, so that the steel-barred cage could be set in place before the show started. The closing act was usually the "Elephant Act," because the ring needed to be shoveled up after it was over.

Elephants were an invaluable part of the circus. Not only did they perform but they were used to move equipment and to erect and dismantle the big top. Although they were all called "bulls," most performing elephants were females, because they were easier to train and were less inclined to throw temper tantrums.

The Grand Headmaster of Elephants was Walter McClain, and during the act that was known as the "Congress of Elephants," he had thirty-six of the lumbering creatures capering about in three rings.

Despite their brute strength, elephants had such sensitive hides they could feel a fly land on them. But because their hair was too tough to be cut with razors, their caretakers, who were called "bull men," had to shave them with blowtorches. They were heavy eaters who consumed one hundred pounds of hay and one hundred gallons of water daily. There was always one "queen" of the elephants who acted as their leader, and the others would obediently fall in behind her. She was also the disciplinarian, and if the other elephants misbehaved, she punished the culprits by butting them with her head.

Training elephants took patience, although their tricks were comparatively simple ones such as sitting down, standing on their front or back legs, or climbing up on a pedestal that was known as a "bull tub." Their most impressive trick was to hold show girls with their trunks and to spin around without crushing them or sending them hurtling off into space like missiles.

After John Ringling's death his nephew, John Ringling North, took over the presidency of the circus, and in 1941 North got the idea for an elephant ballet. He decided he wanted it choreographed by George Balanchine with original music by Igor Stravinsky.

When he phoned Stravinsky to ask if he would "do a little ballet for me—a polka, perhaps—for some elephants?" the famous composer asked, "How old?"

"Very young," North assured him.

"All right. If they are very young elephants, I will do it," Stravinsky responded. And he did.

The "Ballet of the Elephants" was performed by fifty elephants and fifty pretty show girls. The act rehearsed for months at the winter quarters and opened in Madison Square Garden the following spring. It was greeted with such enthusiasm by the audience that it was continued for 425 performances. Few people realized the elephants weren't dancing to the music. What they really were doing was following the direction of their trainer, and the band was keeping time to their movements.

OPPOSITE: A mother elephant and her calf practice leg lifts side by side. Other elephants balance on "bull tubs."

Among the most famous of the attractions at Ringling Bros. was the ferocious gorilla, Gargantua, and his "lovely wife," Toto.

Gargantua was brought over from Africa as an infant by the captain of a freighter, who named the thirty-five-pound baby gorilla "Buddy" and hoped to make a fortune by selling him to a zoo. Just before the ship docked a sailor with a grudge against the captain threw nitric acid on Buddy and drastically disfigured him. The captain ended up selling the badly burned animal to a woman named Gertrude Lintz of Brooklyn, New York. Mrs. Lintz nursed Buddy back to health and treated him like a child, teaching him to dress himself, ride around on a kiddie car, and bring her things from the kitchen. Even when he reached a weight of four hundred pounds, she didn't realize he was dangerous until the day he was affectionately stroking his kitten and crushed its skull.

Then Mrs. Lintz got frightened and sold him to Ringling Bros.

John North's brother Henry was also called "Buddy," and North didn't much like the idea of calling a grotesquely scarred gorilla by his own brother's nickname, so he rechristened Buddy "Gargantua." Since gorillas didn't usually survive very long in captivity, North decided to protect his investment by housing Gargantua in an air-conditioned, germ-free cage. He furnished it with chairs and a swing, but Gargantua was so furious at being confined that he smashed all his furniture. He eventually became so violent that North issued orders that if the gorilla was ever to get loose as the result of a train wreck, he was to be shot without any effort to recapture him.

Gargantua and Toto toured in separate cages, each with two compartments so the occupant could be shut in one end while the other end was cleaned.

In the hope that Gargantua would be happier if he had a companion, North found him a mate. The female gorilla, Toto, had been raised by a woman named Mrs. Hoyt. One day when the two were playing outside in the garden, a friend dropped by unexpectedly. Afraid the intruder might be going to attack her mistress, Toto grabbed Mrs. Hoyt by her hands to whisk her to safety, breaking both the woman's wrists in the process.

Mrs. Hoyt decided her pet had become too much for her and sold her to the circus.

John North planned a highly publicized, formal wedding for the seemingly well-matched couple, but they didn't have a honeymoon. Gargantua greeted his bride by offering her a celery stick, but Toto hurled it back in his face and started jumping up and down, spitting and shrieking. Poor Gargantua was devastated.

Throughout their "marriage" the gorillas lived in separate cages. Even so, Gargantua was a jealous husband. According to one story, when Mrs. Hoyt paid a visit to Toto, Gargantua reached through the bars of his cage and ripped off her dress, leaving her screaming in terror, wearing nothing but her underwear.

If the aerialists were the wings of the circus and the animal acts were its backbone, the heart of the circus most certainly had to be the clowns.

The section of the circus lot where the clowns had their dressing tents was called Clown Alley. Usually it was near the back entrance of the big top, so if an accident should occur during the course of a performance the ringmaster could "send in the clowns" to distract the audience.

Four famous clowns (clockwise from left): Felix Adler, Emmett Kelly, Harry Dann, and Paul Jerome.

Lou Jacobs was considered the King of the White Face Clowns. He was also called The White House Clown because he was often invited into the presidential box when the show played in Washington, D.C.

Charlie Bell enjoyed performing with his pet fox terrier. In his famous hunting routine he would dress the dog in a rabbit costume and chase him around the ring with a shotgun.

It was in Clown Alley that the clowns applied the makeup that transformed them from everyday people into creatures of wonder. The face and props of each clown were his own special trademark, and it was an unwritten law that no other clown could use them. This policy was so well established that the most famous clowns willed their "faces" and professional personalities to their children and grandchildren.

Felix Adler had a bright red nose that lit up.

Harry Dann carried around a pet goose.

Charlie Bell performed with a fox terrier that was dressed as a rabbit.

Lou Jacobs rode around the arena in a motorized bathtub, so that he could bathe while he drove.

Even after the deaths of these beloved performers, no other clowns incorporated those gimmicks into their acts.

There were three basic types of clowns. The most traditional clown was the "White Face," who appeared in white makeup accentuated by black and red features. The second type of clown, the "Auguste," had exaggerated, cartoonlike facial features and was the butt of the other clowns' jokes. The third clown type was the "Character Clown" or "Tramp Clown," who dressed like a hobo and interacted with the audience.

Weather could create problems when the clowns applied makeup. When it was hot, clown white, which was a mixture of grease and zinc oxide, became gummy and sticky, and putty noses softened and wouldn't hold their shape. On cold days clown white stiffened and noses solidified and were hard to take off. Winter in Florida was a clown's idea of paradise, because the weather was mild and temperate, and makeup went on easily.

Lou Jacobs was a contortionist, and his most famous act was to cram his six-foot-one-inch body into a midget car that was designed for him by George Wallenda. Jacobs wore a pair of gigantic shoes, so the first thing the audience saw when he got out of the car was an enormous foot that filled the entire doorway. Jacobs's makeup was so elaborate it took thirty minutes to apply and twenty minutes to remove, a ritual the circus children loved to watch.

BELOW: The two blond children on the left are Carla Wallenda and her little brother, Mario, who was later severely injured in a fall from the high wire.

OPPOSITE: Carla Wallenda eyes Lou Jacobs's early stage of makeup application.

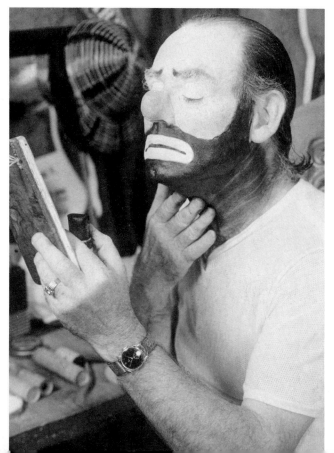

Emmett Kelly was the greatest pantomime circus clown of all time. He played "Weary Willie," a hobo clown whose sorrowful expression never changed, a pathetic bumbler who came out the loser in every situation. His best-known act was to sweep up a spotlight. He swept from the outside inward, and the circle of light grew smaller and smaller, until it was only a dot that Kelly carefully swept into a dustpan.

OPPOSITE: Joseph Steinmetz took this picture for Emmett Kelly to use on his Christmas card. On tour clowns were traditionally given two pails of cold water to wash up in. A bubble bath was a luxury they could enjoy only at home.

The circus people became part of the Sarasota community. When the giant went to the movies, nobody yelled, "Down in front!" Waiters in restaurants brought phone books for the midgets to sit on. The Tattooed Lady strolled the beaches in her two-piece bathing suit, and nobody stared at her. If the air always smelled a little like elephants, nobody complained, and the roar of lions seemed as natural as the roar of the surf.

At school the circus children took over the gym classes, doing cartwheels the length of the football field and staging balancing acts on the goal posts, while the rest of the students watched in awe and then tried to imitate them. Eventually this led to a high school sport called "circus," with performers from Ringling Bros. acting as coaches. Student athletes could win their letters in "circus" by performing as acrobats, trapeze artists, bareback riders, and wire walkers. Each spring the school put on a three-hour performance with jugglers, clowns, and aerialists, and on one occasion, even a "Cat Act" starring a teenage animal trainer.

An ever-changing cast of students from Sarasota High School has been staging "circus" performances for over forty years, inspired by professional Ringling Bros. circus performers like these.

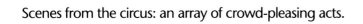

Scenes from the circus: an array of crowd-pleasing acts.

Antoinette Concello, considered by many to be the best woman flyer in circus history, mends her spangled costume in preparation for the upcoming season.

BELOW: Peter Arno, Ringling Bros. art director, uses the winter months to design the circus program, posters, and costumes.

ABOVE AND NEXT PAGE: The big top weighed twenty-one tons when dry, sixty-three tons when wet, and required seventy-three miles of rope. The reason the tent burned so rapidly in 1944 was that the canvas had been coated with a waterproofing solution of benzene and paraffin.

But one of the things about magic is that it's fragile and fleeting. As spring approached, the circus prepared to go on tour again. There were many things to be done before that could happen, including the renovation of over seventy thousand tons of equipment, the inoculation of hundreds of animals, and the mending or replacement of gigantic wardrobes of elaborate costumes.

The most important and time-consuming job was the reconstruction of the big top out of seventy-four thousand yards of fireproof canvas. The two most terrible events in circus history occurred during the Second World War, when the circus couldn't get chemicals to fireproof the tents.

The first of these tragedies took place in Cleveland, Ohio, on August 4, 1942, when a teenage roustabout deliberately set fire to the menagerie tent. Flames roared through the cages that held the helpless, panic-stricken animals, leaving a blackened trail of agony and destruction. The elephants weren't confined and might all have been saved, but they stubbornly refused to leave the tent until their trainer arrived to lead them out. Four elephants died, and others were severely burned. A total of sixty-five animals perished in that fire.

The experience was so horrible that John North wanted to retire the circus until the war was over. His partners voted him down.

Then, on July 6, 1944, in Hartford, Connecticut, the big top itself caught fire during a matinee performance. Once again the arson was the work of a roustabout. This one had been setting fires since the age of six.

Merle Evans, the band leader, was the first to notice a flame snaking up a rope. He signaled the band to start playing the circus disaster song, "The Stars and Stripes Forever," as a signal that there was trouble and the tent must be cleared. When they realized the canvas was on fire, the audience panicked, and six thousand people stampeded wildly for the main exit, which was blocked by the heavy chute that led to the lions' cage.

The huge tent burned to the ground in less than five minutes, leaving 168 people dead and 487 injured. From that time on, no chances were taken with the big top. A new tent was made each year, and it always was fireproofed.

In April the circus staged a farewell performance at the winter quarters. Then they loaded the four long sections of the train with everything they would need for seven months on the road. Animals were transferred from their winter cages into wagons that were lashed onto flat cars. The giraffes traveled in cars with padded ceilings to protect their delicate necks.

John Ringling North and his family had their own railroad car, the Jomar, named for John and his first wife, Mable, with an *R* tacked on for "Ringling." The Jomar was the longest private train car in the world and had a sitting room with a bar, two large staterooms with a connecting bathroom, a dining room, a serving pantry, a kitchen, and living quarters for a chef and valet.

OPPOSITE: Emmett Kelly is "down in the dumps" about leaving winter quarters. He mopes in the circus dump among the discarded wagon wheels from renovated circus wagons.

BELOW: The circus prepares to go back on the road again.

The sixteen hundred troupers of the Ringling Bros. and Barnum & Bailey Circus pack up for another seven-month-long, twenty-thousand-mile tour.

The day the circus left for Madison Square Garden everybody in town turned out to say good-bye. Well-wishers lined the tracks, waving and cheering as a priest blessed the train in Latin and sprinkled it with holy water. When the caboose of the final section disappeared in the distance, the town seemed suddenly small and quiet and boring. Adults returned to their jobs and children to school, and started counting the months until the circus came home again.

As a child I took it for granted the railroad circus would be with us forever, but I was wrong.

In 1956 it came to an end.

One of the reasons for that was an increase in freight rates that tripled the cost of transporting the circus cross-country. Another was a population explosion that made it hard to find space in which to set up the big top. But the death blow was dealt by the popularization of television, for when people had canned entertainment available in their living rooms, they were no longer willing to make the effort to drive across town to sit in a tent.

Ticket sales dropped until the Greatest Show on Earth became history.

Year-round residents of Sarasota gather to wish "their" circus a successful tour.

John Ringling North looks on as Catholic priest Father Elslander, flanked by two acolytes, blesses the circus train in Latin and sprinkles it with holy water as the circus prepares to depart.

At the end of the final performance under the big top, John Ringling North announced sadly, "The tented circus as it exists today is, in my opinion, a thing of the past."

That doesn't mean that there aren't still circuses in existence. There are, but they function today in a very different manner. They travel by truck and perform in coliseums and arenas, and there aren't very many that can afford to maintain a menagerie. The owners of many of these small, mobile circuses are descendants of the very same families who were stars of the big top, and the walls of their homes are covered with my father's photographs of floats and parades and tigers and dancing elephants.

And in Sarasota there still are people who remember. In the evenings they sit on their terraces, watching the sun slide into the gulf as the clouds take on the red and gold of calliope wagons.

"Remember how the soot blew in through the train windows?"

"Remember when the littlest Wallenda girl pretended she was a midget and went on with the Doll family?"

"Remember when a tiger escaped in Madison Square Garden and a clown chased him out of the lobby?"

Hardships and tragedies have no place in these memories as wrinkled faces smile and old voices grow dreamy, recalling a life that was fashioned of sawdust and stardust.

Once upon a time...when there was magic in our land.

Index